THE LIVING GOSPEL

Daily Devotions for Advent 2016

Ann M. Garrido

Ave Maria Press AVE Notre Dame, Indiana

Founded in 1865, Ave Maria Press is a ministry of the United States Province of Holy Cross.

www.avemariapress.com

Paperback: ISBN-13 978-1-59471-703-1

E-book: ISBN-13 978-1-59471-704-8

Cover image "Approaching Bethlehem" © 2012 by Jeni Butler, artworkbyjeni.wix.com/art.

Cover and text design by John R. Carson.

Printed and bound in the United States of America.

INTRODUCTION

God has a dream for our planet, and it is no small matter. God imagines our earth as a place where life flourishes: a place of justice for all peoples and a place of harmony for all creation. In God's dream, those who are blind are given sight, those who are deaf are able to hear, and those who are bound are set free. The hungry are satisfied. The outcasts are welcomed. There are no obstacles to enjoying true communion with one another.

The prophets illustrated this dream for us in rich images drawn from their desert homeland. Images of mountaintop banquets and wolves dining alongside lambs. Jesus made this dream come alive in his preaching and miracles, and he gave this dream a name: in the Greek of the gospels, *Basileia tou Theou*. Or, as we translate in English, "the kingdom of God."

We have not yet experienced this kingdom in its fullness. The earth that we know continues to struggle with violence and war, injustice and hunger. Indeed, we sometimes wonder whether at this point in history it is even possible to forgive, to make needed changes, to be saved as a planet.

And so each year—in the darkest time of year—the Church marks the season of Advent as a time to nourish hope. During these four weeks, we open the Word of God to hear anew of God's dream lest we become discouraged and forget that God does have a vision. Lest we become cavalier and forget that God eagerly awaits our participation to realize this vision. The kingdom of God will not come without us.

The Word of God is a powerful thing. In the book of the prophet Isaiah, God's Word is compared to the rain and snow which does not return to the heavens before it has watered the earth and made it fruitful. "So shall my word be," God says. "It shall not return to me void, but shall do my will, achieving the end for which I sent it" (Is 55:11). When we sit with God's Word and allow it to work within us, we begin to dream the dreams that God dreams. We begin to long for the world God envisions. And we begin to discover the ways that we can participate in bringing this kingdom about.

If you have picked up this booklet, my guess is that you are someone who takes the season of Advent quite seriously. You want to be a person of the Word, and you hope that your prayer during these sacred weeks will lead you to a deeper understanding of that Word. My prayer is that you find these daily reflections helpful in that journey. Come Christmas morn, may we as a Church stand together in awe of the goodness of a God who dreams so much for us that he sent his only Son to show us the way.

Brothers and sisters:
You know the time;
it is the hour now for you to awake from sleep.
For our salvation is nearer now than when we
first believed; the night is advanced, the day is
at hand.

~*Romans 13:11–12*

Sunday, November 27
First Week of Advent

BEGIN

Be silent. Be still. Pray, "Come, Lord Jesus!"

PRAY

I rejoiced because they said to me, "We will go up to the house of the Lord."

~Psalm 122:1

LISTEN

Read Matthew 24:36–44.

Keep awake therefore, for you do not know on what day your Lord is coming.

~Matthew 24:42

What Are We Waiting For?

Has it ever struck you as strange? Each year as we begin this season of preparation before the feast of Christmas, the gospel of the day speaks of the end of the world. What does the final judgment have to do with babies in mangers? What do the four horsemen of the apocalypse have to do with angels singing "Glory to God"? Throughout the history of the Church, these events—the coming of Christ at Bethlehem and the Second Coming—have always been understood as integrally related. When we say we are preparing for the advent of Christ each year, we are not pretending to go back in time to get ready for Jesus' historical birth. We are not throwing a nice birthday party for Jesus. We are doing something that demands so much more of us. We are readying ourselves for the end of time when, St. Paul says, God will "be all in all" (1 Cor 15:28). When God's presence will fill all of creation like God's presence filled the person of Jesus.

We don't know when that day will be. As today's gospel passage from Matthew warns, no one knows. But what we do know is that Christ's Second Coming has something to do with our response to Christ's first coming. It has something to do with whether we are truly living into our vocation as the Body of Christ in our time. "What good is it that Christ was born two thousand years ago," asks the thirteenth century German mystic Meister Eckhart, "if he is not born now in your heart?" Indeed, it is misleading to speak of Christ's Second Coming for in reality what we are waiting for "is the fulfillment of his one coming which is still in progress at the present time," as Jesuit priest and theologian Karl Rahner wrote. How will you participate in the coming of Christ this year?

ACT

Consider one thing you could do today that would make Christ more present in your own home or workplace. Then do it.

PRAY

Come, Lord Jesus, and be born in my heart anew this Advent season.

MONDAY, NOVEMBER 28
FIRST WEEK OF ADVENT

BEGIN

Be silent. Be still. Pray, "Come, Lord Jesus!"

PRAY

I rejoiced because they said to me, "We will go up to
the house of the LORD."

~Psalm 122:1

LISTEN

Read Matthew 8:5–11.

The centurion said in reply, "Lord, I am not worthy to
have you enter under my roof; only say the word and
my servant will be healed."

~Matthew 8:8

The Power of Word

Each year the season of Advent begins with recounting a
dialogue that took place between Jesus and a centurion
in Capernaum. A centurion was a Roman army leader
who oversaw upwards of one hundred soldiers. He was
a man of significant influence, personally responsible for
the training and discipline of his troops. When he spoke,
others listened. Things happened. If they did not, pun-
ishment could be swift and harsh. His word had behind
it all the force of Rome.

The centurion recognizes that Jesus' word is also
very powerful. Like God at the dawn of creation, when
Jesus speaks things come to be. Saying it equals doing it.
A promise made is a promise kept. And it is the centurion's knowledge of the power of words in his own life

that leads him to trust that what Jesus says will happen. Jesus' word has all the power of God behind it.

In our own lives, perhaps we've not had this experience of speech equaling action. We know words that have been cheap, untrue, and unfaithful, making it hard to trust in the power of words. But, as we begin Advent with a Bible in our lap, we are issued an invitation to trust anew in the power of God's Word. We are promised that if we sit with *this* Word, we will know healing and renewal. The Word we will hear in these coming weeks will remind us of visions seen and visions realized, promises made and promises kept. If we can steep ourselves in *this* Word, we will be different people at the end of Advent than we are right now. And we, too, will greet Christ on Christmas morn with a centurion's confidence.

ACT

Practice integrity in your own speech today, careful to say yes only when you mean yes and no only when you mean no—making promises only that you can and will keep.

PRAY

Jesus, teach me the power of your Word this day.

Tuesday, November 29
First Week of Advent

BEGIN

Be silent. Be still. Pray, "Come, Lord Jesus!"

PRAY

May his name be blessed forever; as long as the sun
his name shall remain.

~Psalm 72:17

LISTEN

Read Isaiah 11:1–10.

A shoot shall sprout from the stump of Jesse, and
from his roots a bud shall blossom. The Spirit of the
LORD shall rest upon him: a Spirit of wisdom and
understanding, a Spirit of counsel and of strength, a
Spirit of knowledge and of fear of the LORD, and his
delight shall be the fear of the LORD.

~Isaiah 11:1–3a

Who Notices the Shoot?

Isaiah 10 closes with God hacking through the forests
of Lebanon with an ax, lopping down the tallest of trees
with "terrifying power." It would seem that this once
majestic woodland has come to an end. It has been
wiped out. But then begins Isaiah 11. In the midst of all
of the destruction comes a shoot—a tiny burst of green.
From what appears to be dead, new life emerges. And
although this new life is fragile and hidden, the fullness
of God's Spirit rests upon it, filling it with every good
gift.

In this image, Isaiah illumines a pattern that weaves through all of scripture: God showing a "preferential option" for the small. We see it over and over again. Of all the peoples of the earth, God chooses to make a covenant with tiny, insignificant Israel. Of all the possible kings for Israel, God chooses David, the youngest son of Jesse who is out in the field caring for sheep. Of all the places for the Messiah to be born, God chooses the little village of Bethlehem. Of all the places in Bethlehem to be born, God picks a manger. God's Spirit rests on the little ones of the earth, and it is here that God's power is most visible.

Today's newspapers are filled with stories of the mighty falling. The streaming ribbon across the bottom of the TV screen bears continual updates of death and destruction. "Who would not notice a forest falling with a crash? Who would not be captivated by the noise and destruction?" asks the Italian biblical scholar Sofia Cavalletti. "Yet have you ever noticed when a little shoot begins to spring forth?" What captivates *your* attention? What *could* captivate your attention?

ACT

Today pay special attention to someone or something "small" to see how God might be at work there: Donate to a little-known charity. Converse with a young child. Skim the newspaper for a "good news" story and hang it on your refrigerator.

PRAY

Mighty God, awaken within me an awareness of where you are at work in the tiny, hidden places of life.

WEDNESDAY, NOVEMBER 30
FIRST WEEK OF ADVENT

BEGIN

Be silent. Be still. Pray, "Come, Lord Jesus!"

PRAY

You spread the table before me. . . . My cup
overflows.

~Psalm 23:5

LISTEN

Read Matthew 15:29–37.

Jesus walked by the Sea of Galilee, went up on the
mountain, and sat down there. . . . Jesus summoned
his disciples and said, "My heart is moved with pity
for the crowd, for they have been with me now for
three days and have nothing to eat. I do not want to
send them away hungry."

~Matthew 15:29, 32

The Kingdom Is a Feast

In today's first reading, the prophet Isaiah paints a picture of what the world will be like when God's dreams
for planet Earth are realized: all will come to God's holy
mountain for a feast of rich foods and fine wines. In
today's gospel, a crowd gathers around Jesus on a mountaintop, and he feeds them with an abundance of loaves
and fish. Coincidence? No. As we will see time and
again, the Lectionary readings of Advent are arranged
in such a way to illumine for us what St. Augustine calls
the "golden thread" that unites the words of the prophets to our experience of Jesus and to our ongoing hopes

and dreams for what God's kingdom will look like in its fullness at the end of time.

One of the threads that we can trace throughout history is that God cares a great deal about human hunger. The prophets and sages allude to it constantly. Jesus' ministry repeatedly finds him eating with or feeding others. We have yet to see that day when *all* will have their hungers satiated on God's holy mountain. But we have seen signs of it. And we who live in this time in between Christ's first coming in Bethlehem and Christ's Second Coming at the end of time know that *we* are part of this history. In this "in between time," we are nourished by Christ's Body in the Eucharist that we might become Christ's Body in a still hungry world. God continues to care about human hunger.

ACT

Take your place in the "golden thread" today by participating in God's ongoing concern for human hunger: Make a donation to a food pantry. Invite someone over for dinner. Bring a meal to a family going through a tough time.

PRAY

O, Lord, feed the deepest hungers of my mind, heart, and body.

Thursday, December 1
First Week of Advent

BEGIN

Be silent. Be still. Pray, "Come, Lord Jesus!"

PRAY

Trust in the Lord forever! For the Lord is an eternal Rock.

~Isaiah 26:4

LISTEN

Read Matthew 7:21, 24–27.

Everyone who listens to these words of mine and acts on them will be like a wise man who built his house on rock.

~Matthew 7:24

God's Word Is a Rock

Last year, I had the gift of visiting a town along the southern coastline of Mississippi. Ten years after Hurricane Katrina, there was still some evidence of the destruction wrought by the storm: a twisted slide descending into a swimming pool now covered in mud and grass as well as a set of stairs leading to nowhere. But all along my morning walking path were also new homes set atop concrete pillars twenty, even thirty feet high. They looked like tree houses but perched higher than the surrounding trees. Here were people who knew the potential power of wind and rain and weren't going to be caught unaware again. They had constructed homes built to survive storms.

In today's first reading, God is compared to an "eternal Rock" by Isaiah. And in the gospel passage from Matthew, Jesus says that those who listen to his words will be like those who build on solid ground. Though the winds of change blow and life floods us with more than we feel we can handle, he promised that those rooted in his Word would experience stability even in the midst of storms. Note that Jesus doesn't promise that there won't be storms. Sometimes we are tempted to believe that if we are "good people" who try to follow God's Word, bad things won't happen to us. They still do. But those rooted in God's Word will find a strength that others can only marvel at.

Do you experience God's Word as a strength in your life? What would it look like to be even more firmly grounded in the Word this Advent season?

ACT

Talk to someone today who you consider to be deeply grounded in the Word of God, and ask them to share a time when sitting with scripture made a difference in their life.

PRAY

Be my eternal Rock, O Lord, in the storms of life.

Friday, December 2
First Week of Advent

BEGIN

Be silent. Be still. Pray, "Come, Lord Jesus!"

PRAY

One thing I ask of the LORD . . . that I may gaze on the loveliness of the LORD.

~Psalm 27:4

LISTEN

Read Matthew 9:27–31.

As Jesus passed by, two blind men followed him, crying out "Son of David, have pity on us!" When he entered the house, the blind men approached him and Jesus said to them, "Do you believe that I can do this?"

~Matthew 9:27–28

The Eyes of the Blind Shall See

In today's first reading from Isaiah 29, the prophet offers another image of what life will look like in the fullness of God's kingdom: "out of the gloom and darkness, the eyes of the blind shall see." In the gospel, two men who are blind cry out to Jesus for help. He asks whether they believe that he has the power to heal them. They do, and he does.

Sometimes when we read the miracle stories in scripture, Jesus comes across as a magician with special powers, arbitrarily making the lives of a few better while many in the world continue to suffer. We wonder why such wonders don't happen today, and we question whether it is lack of belief. If we had more faith, would we get miracles, too?

It seems important to read these stories as the gospel writers intended—within the context of Jesus' broader ministry. Jesus' whole life was about proclaiming the kingdom of God. He preached about it ceaselessly, prayed for it to come, and sometimes gave us signs as to what it would look like. Indeed, wherever Jesus goes the kingdom of God seems to break out. The healing of the two blind men is an example of that. In their newfound sight, we get a glimpse of where all of history is headed.

Just as God cares deeply about human hunger, God also cares deeply about humans' ability to see—physically, spiritually, intellectually. And while we have not yet seen all that God has in store for us, we continue to experience God's ministry of illumination in the work of medical professionals, teachers, preachers, and writers. The "golden thread" of God's care continues.

ACT

Participate in God's "golden thread" of concern for "sight" today: Make a donation to a charity that makes a difference in the lives of those who are blind. Volunteer as a reading partner at a local school. Spend time listening to someone who is struggling with meaning in their life right now.

PRAY

Illumine the path you would have me walk, O Lord.

Saturday, December 3
First Week of Advent

BEGIN

Be silent. Be still. Pray, "Come, Lord Jesus!"

PRAY

Praise the LORD, for he is good; sing praise to our
God, for he is gracious.

~Psalm 147:1

LISTEN

Read Matthew 9:35–10:6.

At the sight of the crowds, his heart was moved
with pity for them because they were troubled and
abandoned, like sheep without a shepherd. Then he
said to his disciples, "The harvest is abundant but the
laborers are few; so ask the master of the harvest to
send out laborers for his harvest."

~Matthew 9:36–38

The Sheep Will Have a Shepherd

At varying places throughout the Old Testament, God
expresses his great dismay that the leaders of the people
are not shepherding the flock as he would. In a particularly poignant passage in Ezekiel, spoken in the time of
the Babylonian exile, God bemoans that under self-serving leaders his sheep have been scattered across the
earth, separated from one another, left vulnerable and
alone. God promises there will come a time when God
himself will shepherd them, binding up their wounds,
and leading them home. In one of the darkest hours in
Jewish history, a dream is born among the people: "What

will it be like when God is our shepherd? When God reigns?"

Like the prophets before him, Jesus shares this dream of what earth will be like when God reigns. Everywhere he goes, today's gospel reiterates, he proclaims the kingdom of God. And he finds that the crowds to whom he is speaking share his passion. They long for the kingdom as much as he does. They constantly bring him their hurting. They hang on his every word. Jesus acts as the shepherd they have waited for. But the needs are overwhelming; the longing for God's Word is overpowering. The kingdom of God needs helpers.

In the United States, we have just been through another bruising electoral cycle, and it is easy for us to critique our leaders as self-serving and ineffectual. It is much harder to participate in the "golden thread" of God's leadership and share in the work of shepherding—seeking out the lost, uniting the scattered, binding up wounds. Yet that is what the gospel asks of us today: to be the kinds of leaders we want to see.

ACT

> Make one proactive move today to bring together a group that is scattered or divided: Reach out for coffee with someone who votes differently than you. Plan a shared meal among people who are strangers. Visit a homebound neighbor with a treat.

PRAY

> Shepherd me, O Lord, into the ministry of shepherding.

Sunday, December 4

Second Week of Advent

BEGIN

Be silent. Be still. Pray, "Come, Lord Jesus!"

PRAY

May his name be blessed forever. . . . In him shall all
the tribes of the earth be blessed; all the nations shall
proclaim his happiness.

~Psalm 72:17

LISTEN

Read Matthew 3:1–12.

John the Baptist appeared, preaching in the desert
of Judea and saying, "Repent, for the kingdom of
heaven is at hand!" It was of him that the prophet
Isaiah had said: *A voice of one crying out in the desert,
"Prepare the way of the Lord, make straight his paths."*

~Matthew 3:1–3

John Prepares the Way

In the readings of the first week of Advent, we heard the
visionary words of the prophets imagining the kingdom
of God. We heard the powerful words of Jesus announc-
ing the dawning of that kingdom and giving signs of
its realization. And we heard Jesus asking God to send
colaborers who share his passion for the kingdom. As
we enter the second week of Advent, we will begin to
meet some of those earliest coworkers in the vineyard,
persons who can model for us what it means to colabor
for the kingdom. The first of those we meet is John.

John was another prophet in the time of Jesus—as different from Jesus as night from day in terms of personality but similar in devotion to the kingdom of God. Jesus and John probably attracted many of the same people and shared many of the same disciples. As popular, charismatic figures, it would have become easy for Jesus and John to enter into competition with each other or be pitted against each other, but the gospel writers emphasize that they were family—that they were pulling in the same direction even if by different means. John's ministry, they assert, prepared for Jesus' ministry. It paved the way, like a road in the desert, for Jesus to come. John awakened people to their sinfulness, helping them to see how far they were from God's dreams for them. He created within them a ravenous hunger to hear Jesus' words of mercy and forgiveness. As you steep yourself in God's Word this Advent season, what does John's message awaken within you? What does it make you long for?

ACT

Take time today for a more thorough examination of conscience, asking God to show you those areas of your life where you are far from God's dreams for you.

PRAY

Awaken within me a sense of sin, O Lord, that I might enjoy more fully your gift of mercy.

Monday, December 5
Second Week of Advent

BEGIN

Be silent. Be still. Pray, "Come, Lord Jesus!"

PRAY

Say to those whose hearts are frightened: Be strong,
fear not! Here is your God.

~Isaiah 35:4

LISTEN

Read Luke 5:17–26.

He said to the one who was paralyzed, "I say to you,
rise, pick up your stretcher, and go home." He stood
up immediately before them, picked up what he had
been lying on, and went home, glorifying God.

~Luke 5:24–25

The Lame Shall Leap

In the first reading today, Isaiah envisions a day when
the "lame will leap like a stag." There will be a "high-
way" called "the holy way." "It is for those with a journey to make," says Isaiah, "and on it the redeemed will
walk." In today's gospel, Jesus heals a man who has been
paralyzed physically and also possibly spiritually. Jesus
not only gives him new use of his legs but also forgives
him of his sin. He frees him to "leap like a stag" and walk
with "the redeemed."

Just as hunger or blindness can be understood meta-
phorically as well as literally, so can paralysis. And here
we discover another one of those "golden threads" that
weave through scripture: God is concerned about human

freedom. God wants us to be able to walk the roads of the neighborhoods in which we live, but God also wants us to be able to walk the journey of life. Freedom to move physically is not unlike the freedom to change and grow without constraint internally, which implies a release from sin and other blockages.

Just as we are nourished by the Eucharist so that we can be the Body of Christ for others and just as we are illumined with the light of Baptism so that we can be light for others, we need release from sin so that we can "walk the talk" with others. The sacrament of Reconciliation is one way that God continues to offer us freedom today. Through the repentance preached by the John the Baptist, we can join the journey toward the kingdom of God.

ACT

Investigate opportunities to participate in the sacrament of Reconciliation during this Advent season.

PRAY

Free me, O Lord, from all that paralyzes me.

Tuesday, December 6
Second Week of Advent

BEGIN

Be silent. Be still. Pray, "Come, Lord Jesus!"

PRAY

Sing to the LORD a new song; sing to the LORD, all you lands.

~Psalm 96:1

LISTEN

Read Isaiah 40:1–11.

Every valley shall be filled in, every mountain and hill shall be made low; the rugged land shall be made a plain, the rough country, a broad valley. Then the glory of the LORD shall be revealed, and all people shall see it together.

~Isaiah 40:4–5

Seeing Together

A few years ago, I experienced the wonders of driving through the Kenai Peninsula of Alaska with a friend who had grown up there. The going was often slow as we wound through the narrow valleys in the shade of mighty mountains. My friend pointed to the riverside property where she had once lived. "What was it like to be a child here?" I asked. "Dark," she replied. It was a happy childhood, but the sense she most remembered was that of living in a perpetual shadow. The mountains blocked out much of the light even in the land of midnight sun.

In today's first reading, Isaiah speaks of a time when mountains will be made low and valleys raised so that the land becomes a plain. I think it is safe to say that Isaiah did not have the environmental catastrophe of mountaintop removal in mind when he wrote but rather a metaphor for what a just earth would look like: there are persons whose lives are bathed in light and offer far reaching views, and there are persons whose lives are wrapped in shadow and can see only to the next bend in the road. In order for God to come quickly, Isaiah says there will need to be some leveling of the terrain. That doesn't necessarily sound like good news for those of us who enjoy mountaintop homes. Who wants to lose a privileged position? But Isaiah names a joy that we rarely experience in our uneven social order: the profound abiding joy of seeing the light of the Lord *together*. A joy, we might suspect, that will more than compensate for any sacrifice we might make for the coming of the kingdom.

ACT

Commit today to one act of "leveling the terrain" through a work of justice that serves either the local or global community.

PRAY

Ignite within me, O Lord, the passion for justice that precedes the joy of your coming.

Wednesday, December 7
Second Week of Advent

BEGIN

Be silent. Be still. Pray, "Come, Lord Jesus!"

PRAY

They that hope in the Lord will renew their strength,
they will soar as with eagles' wings.

~Isaiah 40:30

LISTEN

Read Matthew 11:28–30.

Come to me, all you who labor and are burdened,
and I will give you rest. Take my yoke upon you and
learn from me, for I am meek and humble of heart;
and you will find rest for yourselves.

~Matthew 11:28–29

The Weary Shall Rest

Are you tired yet? Weary of circling the parking lots of shopping centers listening to an endless litany of Christmas commercials punctuated by the same six carols? Frazzled by to-do lists longer than Santa's? It seems unfair that during the month when we most long for extra hours in the day, the sun insists on setting earlier and earlier.

Since beginning the Advent season, the readings have highlighted some of God's dearest dreams for us: nourishment, sight, and freedom. Today we hear another: rest. The prophet Isaiah envisions a time when we will "run and not grow weary, walk and not grow faint," a time when we shall "soar as with eagles' wings."

Jesus beckons, "Come . . . I will give you rest." Is it really possible that God values renewal, relaxation, and sleep in the same way God values nourishment, sight, and freedom? Yes. This is the same God who declared the Sabbath in the first week of creation. Who named the Sabbath in the first ten commands on Mt. Sinai. Who brings it up again over a hundred times in the Hebrew scriptures. But when is the last time that we took the third commandment seriously when examining our consciences? For some reason, this is the commandment most of us find justifiable to dismiss.

Today's readings ask us to take rest far more seriously, even in the midst of this hurried season. Strange as it sounds, one of the ways we prepare for the kingdom of God is to practice not doing anything at all.

ACT

Spend at least a half hour today doing something that you find restful and renewing: playing a board game, lying quietly on the couch, reading in silence, etc.

PRAY

Show me, O Gentle One, what it would mean to rest in you.

Thursday, December 8
Second Week of Advent
Feast of the Immaculate Conception

BEGIN

Be silent. Be still. Pray, "Come, Lord Jesus!"

PRAY

Sing to the LORD a new song, for he has done wondrous deeds.

~Psalm 98:1

LISTEN

Read Luke 1:26–38.

Then the angel said to her, "Do not be afraid, Mary, for you have found favor with God."

~Luke 1:30

A Healing at the Root

In the words of St. Augustine, "Our hearts are restless until they rest in You, O Lord." We are wired from the beginning to be in relationship with God. But how do we learn what relationship looks like and how it works? From our parents, of course. Even within the womb, we can hear the voices of our mother and father. We can feel the quickening of our mother's pulse when she is afraid or the tensing of her muscles when she is angry. By the time we are born, certain patterns of relating and reacting are already conditioned. As the philosopher René Girard noted, we relate by imitating the relationships we are born into. However, not all of those relationships are right relationships—indeed, none are untouched by sin. The first relationships we ever imitate are already flawed ones.

But for Jesus this was not the case. Even before he was born, his muscles and memories were being formed in the womb of one who was and had always been in right relationship. As he learned how to relate, he imitated the patterns of one without sin. When the Church lifts up the Immaculate Conception of Mary, it is claiming that in advance of Jesus' coming, God healed the chronic human orientation toward sin at the root. God oriented Mary to right relationship from the beginning of her life so that she could in turn provide that orientation for Jesus, that he might never suffer a restless heart.

ACT

Reflect on the patterns of relating that you learned from your own family life. How have these patterns helped you to be a better friend, spouse, community member? And how have they sometimes hindered or fractured important relationships?

PRAY

Through the intercession of Mary, O Lord, may I learn the secrets of right relationship with you.

Friday, December 9
Second Week of Advent

BEGIN

Be silent. Be still. Pray, "Come, Lord Jesus!"

PRAY

Blessed the man who . . . delights in the law of the
Lord and meditates on his law day and night.

~*Psalm 1:1–2*

LISTEN

Read Matthew 11:16–19.

For John came neither eating nor drinking, and they
said, "He is possessed by a demon." The Son of Man
came eating and drinking and they said, "Look, he
is a glutton and a drunkard, a friend of tax collectors
and sinners."

~*Matthew 11:18–19*

Confronting Our Inner Eeyore

All of us have an Eeyore in our lives. Someone who, no
matter how we try to make them happy, is determined
not to be. Someone who readily points out all the rea-
sons something won't work. Who finds fault with every
suggestion. Who is quick to critique but never lifts a
finger to help.

Jesus seems to have encountered plenty of Eeyores
in his ministry and, as today's gospel records, he clearly
found them frustrating. John's way of proclaiming and
living the kingdom of God didn't work for them, and
now Jesus' way doesn't either. No matter how Jesus
adapts the tune, no one wants to dance.

We can empathize with Jesus, until we pause to wonder whether Jesus continues his lament unto today. Across the globe right now, there are thousands of mustard-seed efforts to make the kingdom of God more real: the kid who wants to sell lemonade for world peace, the parishioner with a new idea, the one-person lobby trying to influence a huge societal issue, and the Salvation Army musician banging on his kettle. Two thousand years down the road from today's gospel, we get where the people of Jesus' day were coming from. We suffer compassion fatigue. We suspect nothing we do will make a real difference. But in our own eyes, we're not Eeyore; *we* are just being realistic, reasonable, and appropriately suspicious.

Jesus' words today invite us to check our own pessimism about the coming kingdom of God. Do we still believe that what God dreams for our planet can be realized? Are we still willing to contribute as we are able to bring the kingdom about? How will we support those fresh in their hope?

ACT

Lend your support today to one person who is committed to a great good even if you perceive their efforts to be a bit naïve.

PRAY

Fill me anew, O God, with hope for your kingdom.

Saturday, December 10
Second Week of Advent

BEGIN

Be silent. Be still. Pray, "Come, Lord Jesus!"

PRAY

Blessed is he who shall have seen you.

~Sirach 48:11

LISTEN

Read Matthew 17:9–13.

Elijah will indeed come and restore all things; but I tell you that Elijah has already come, and they did not recognize him but did to him whatever they pleased. So also will the Son of Man suffer at their hands.

~Matthew 17:11–12

Coming Down the Mountain

In today's gospel, Jesus and his disciples are "coming down" from a remarkable experience. Literally, they are descending the mountain upon which Jesus had just been transfigured and conversed with Moses and Elijah. But we can also imagine emotionally they are "coming down" from what was surely a spiritual high point in their lives. The disciples inquire about a scholarly debate active in religious circles of their time: the relationship between Elijah and the coming of God's reign. Jesus points them to what is right before their eyes but perhaps they've had a hard time seeing: Elijah *has* come in the person of John the Baptist, and he's been done away with, just as Jesus will be done away with.

Jesus and John were very different persons with different roles in the kingdom of God, but they would both suffer the same fate: death at the hands of those in power. In these hope-filled days of Advent, rich with imagery of what God's kingdom will look like in its fullness, we may experience the shift in tone in today's gospel as a "coming down." Wait, we want to say, doesn't this reading fit better in Lent? But the good news of the kingdom is always tied in some fashion to the paschal mystery. God's kingdom comes about through the mystery of death . . . and, of course, what is not mentioned in this reading but that we know to be true—the mystery of resurrection.

ACT

Take a moment today to be present to someone who is experiencing a down time even in the midst of Advent, someone who is suffering or has lost someone close and is having a hard time enjoying the season.

PRAY

Illumine for me, O Lord, the mystery of death begetting abundant kingdom life.

Sunday, December 11
Third Week of Advent

BEGIN

Be silent. Be still. Pray, "Come, Lord Jesus!"

PRAY

Those whom the LORD has ransomed will . . . meet with joy and gladness, sorrow and mourning will flee.

~Isaiah 35:10

LISTEN

Read Matthew 11:2–11.

When John the Baptist heard in prison of the works of the Christ, he sent his disciples to Jesus with this question, "Are you the one who is to come, or should we look for another?" Jesus said to them in reply, "Go and tell John what you hear and see: the blind regain their sight, the lame walk, lepers are cleansed, the deaf hear, the dead are raised, and the poor have the good news proclaimed to them."

~Matthew 11:2–5

Can You See the Signs?

Imagine for a minute what it must have been like to be John in prison—locked away in a dark cell with an uncertain future and perhaps some despair. What if my life has been a waste? What if this Jesus I've pointed to is not "the one"? In this moment of doubt, Jesus doesn't send John's disciples back with reassuring promises of a yet-unseen future but with their own eyewitness stories of signs of hope that are bursting forth wherever Jesus goes: the blind seeing, the lame walking, the deaf hearing, and more. All of the signs of the kingdom of God that the prophets spoke about so long ago are breaking out in daily life.

Today the Church is garbed in pink—that color of hope in the midst of darkness. We are reminded that even though daylight is difficult to come by and waiting is hard, we are not to cave in to despair but to be open to and sustained by those signs already present in the world around us that let us know God *is* at work. While we have not seen the kingdom of God yet in its fullness, there are ways in which that future is breaking into our own time even now—bursts of illumination and freedom, connection and healing. Our faith does not hinge on promises still unfulfilled but on promises in the process of being fulfilled this very day.

ACT

Have a conversation at the dinner table tonight about what you are seeing right now in the world around you that is giving you hope.

PRAY

Open my eyes, O God, to the mysteries of the kingdom that are present in my midst.

Monday, December 12
Third Week of Advent
Feast of Our Lady of Guadalupe

BEGIN

Be silent. Be still. Pray, "Come, Lord Jesus!"

PRAY

Sing and rejoice, O daughter of Zion! See, I am coming to dwell among you, says the LORD.

~Zechariah 2:14

LISTEN

Read Luke 1:26–38.

And coming to her, he said, "Hail, full of grace! The Lord is with you."

~Luke 1:28

The Lord Is with Us

In today's gospel passage, the angel Gabriel greets Mary with a stunning claim: "The Lord is with you." The mighty God who created the universe and all that is in it, whose embrace stretches beyond the farthest star, is here, now, in your midst. This God is not distant and inaccessible but enters into the limits of the human condition in a way *she* can experience, in whatever language *she* understands, wherever it is that *she* lives.

While the coming of Jesus certainly crystalizes God's desire to dwell among us in a most particular way, we can also say that this desire was not only expressed in the incarnation of Christ. Indeed, it is a theme that permeates scripture and the wider Judeo-Christian tradition.

Throughout history, God always conveys his longing to be *with* people.

Today we celebrate the Feast of Our Lady of Guadalupe, a feast that celebrates God's continued pattern of acting "incarnationally." At a time in history when the Aztec people of modern-day Mexico were feeling diminished and forgotten, Mary heralds God's desire to dwell with them in the midst of their struggle. She comes dressed in *their* clothes, speaking *their* Nahuatl language. She comes looking like *them*.

And this pattern continues today. This God is still "Emmanuel"—still with us, still meeting us in ways we can grasp, still speaking to us in ways we can understand. No culture, no people, no time is excluded from the incarnational impulse of God.

ACT

Ask a Christian from another culture to share a story that is treasured in their tradition about a time in which they knew God was with them.

PRAY

Open my eyes, O Lord, to the ways you are with me right now in the particularities of my life.

TUESDAY, DECEMBER 13
THIRD WEEK OF ADVENT

BEGIN

Be silent. Be still. Pray, "Come, Lord Jesus!"

PRAY

The LORD is close to the broken hearted.

~Psalm 34:19

LISTEN

Read Matthew 21:28–32.

A man had two sons. He came to the first and said, "Son, go out and work in the vineyard today." The son said in reply, "I will not," but afterwards he changed his mind and went. The man came to the other son and gave the same order. He said in reply, "Yes, sir," but did not go. Which of the two did his father's will?

~Matthew 21:28–31

Being Faithful to Our Word

When we began the Advent season, we heard the story of the Roman centurion who believed in the power of Jesus' word. He knew that every word that Jesus spoke was true and that if Jesus *said* something would be, *it would be*. For us, however, it is often not the case. We say we will do one thing, but we do another. We have good intent, but we do not follow through. As a result, the power of our words is cheapened.

As we pass the midpoint of this Advent season, the gospel reading of the day addresses this very conundrum. It suggests that we might want to take a moment to remember the intentions we had two weeks ago when we launched into this season. Are we taking time to marinate in God's Word as we wanted? Are we following through on those prophetic works of justice and mercy that we hoped to do? Are we taking those moments of rest that we promised ourselves in the midst of the holiday craziness?

Today we celebrate the Feast of St. Lucy, a fourth-century martyr who is noted as the patron saint against blindness. Through her intercession, we can ask for illumination of any blindness we might be experiencing right now that hinders us from seeing where our own words and actions are unaligned. What Advent practices do we need to renew our commitment to today?

ACT

Recommit to one practice you had wanted to incorporate into your Advent journey that has been hard to carry through.

PRAY

Through the intercession of St. Lucy, O Lord, make me ever more faithful to what I have said I would do.

Wednesday, December 14
Third Week of Advent

BEGIN

Be silent. Be still. Pray, "Come, Lord Jesus!"

PRAY

The LORD . . . proclaims peace for his people.

~Psalm 85:9

LISTEN

Read Isaiah 45:6–25.

For thus says the LORD, The creator of the heavens,
who is God, the designer and maker of the earth
who established it, not creating it to be a waste, but
designing it be lived in: I am the LORD, and there is no
other.

~Isaiah 45:18

God's Dream for Earth

Sometimes when working with high school students in the past, I'd ask them to draw me a picture of the kingdom of God. Inevitably the first round of artwork would come back with St. Peter standing in front of pearly white gates in clouds. I would then insist that we go back and read Jesus' teaching on the topic again—parables that talk about mustard seeds and pearls and sons coming home and wedding feasts with nary a cloud in view. When Jesus and the prophets speak of the kingdom of God, they are not talking about what God has planned for another realm. They are talking about God's plans for planet Earth, what it will look like when God reigns *here*, as God already reigns in the heavens.

Last year, when Pope Francis released the encyclical *Laudato si'*, he emphasized the same point as Isaiah in today's first reading: the earth was not created "to be a waste" but designed to "be lived in." It is precious to God, the chosen site for God's emerging kingdom. Furthermore, Francis highlights there is an intimate connection between justice and environmental well-being. It is impossible to realize one without the other. The link is so strong in Isaiah's mind that he uses the language of one to describe the other: "Let justice descend like dew from above, like gentle rain let the skies drop it down."

Concern for the earth needs to be part of our Advent practice, just as is concern for the people of the earth. God's dream encompasses both.

ACT

Take a concrete action on behalf of the environment today: make a donation to an environmental action organization, separate out your recyclables, line dry a load of laundry instead of machine drying, carpool to work or to events when possible, reuse an item instead of throwing it away.

PRAY

Teach me gratitude, O Creator, for the wonders of your earth.

Thursday, December 15
Third Week of Advent

BEGIN

Be silent. Be still. Pray, "Come, Lord Jesus!"

PRAY

O Lord, my God, forever will I give you thanks.

~Psalm 30:13

LISTEN

Read Luke 7:24–30.

What did you go out to the desert to see—a reed
swaying in the wind? Then what did you go out to
see? Someone dressed in fine garments? . . . Then
what did you go out to see? A prophet? Yes, I tell you,
and more than a prophet.

~Luke 7:24–26

With Hearts Full of Gratitude

Today's gospel passage immediately follows the passage that we read on Sunday about the disciples of John
who've come at John's request seeking some confirma-
tion of Jesus' identity. As they take leave, Jesus now
turns to the crowds around him and confirms John's
identity. He names what the people already knew in
their guts: there is something special about John. They
hadn't trudged out into the desert to see the scenery;
they had been drawn there by a man on fire with the
Word of God. A man whose ministry had prepared them
for meeting Jesus. One senses in today's reading Jesus'
profound gratitude for John and how highly he thought

of him. Jesus knew he could not have planted the seeds had John not first tilled the soil.

Each of us now on a journey of faith knows that we would not be where we are today without persons who first readied our hearts to receive the Word of God—perhaps a grandmother who taught us to pray in her native tongue, a Sunday school teacher who taught us to sing before we could even read, a parent who locked hands with our own and showed us how to make the Sign of the Cross over our foreheads, lips, and hearts. Perhaps this person emerged later in life—the campus minister who made faith suddenly seem relevant, the preacher whose challenging homily turned our life in a different direction. Today, with Jesus, we can pause to hold these people in our hearts with deep gratitude, for they have been our John the Baptists.

ACT

> Write a note of gratitude to someone from your past who first helped to set your feet on the path toward Christ.

PRAY

> Thank you, O Lord, for all those who have pointed me in your direction.

Friday, December 16
Third Week of Advent

BEGIN

Be silent. Be still. Pray, "Come, Lord Jesus!"

PRAY

May God bless us, and may all the ends of the earth
fear him!

~Psalm 67:8

LISTEN

Read Isaiah 56:1–3, 6–8.

Let not the foreigner say, when he would join himself
to the LORD, "The LORD will surely exclude me from
his people." . . . Thus says the Lord GOD, who gathers
the dispersed of Israel: Others I will gather to him
besides those already gathered.

~Isaiah 56:3, 8

How Far Does His Voice Reach?

One day when my son was still in preschool, he asked
me if I would read him the Christmas story from the
Bible while he moved the figures of our Nativity set.
I was in the midst of doing something, so I told him
to get the figures ready and I would come as soon as I
could. When I arrived, he had the crèche scene set, but
there was our globe in the middle of it. Thinking he was
being silly, I told him the globe needed to go before I
could read. He looked disappointed and returned it to
the shelf. I began to read: "In those days, Caesar Augus-
tus published a decree ordering a census of the whole
world." He tugged my arm, "Now may I get the globe?"

At the age of three, he had already intuited a central theme of the Christian gospel: the coming of Christ has a global significance. Certainly Jesus' first ministry was to his own people. But throughout the gospels, beginning with his birth, we will see that people from beyond Israel's borders were drawn to him: the magi with their gifts, the Syro-Phoenician woman begging for scraps, and the centurion with his ailing servant. Jesus' magnetic message put the whole world on the move.

We who live today can give testimony to the truth of Isaiah's mysterious words from so long ago. Through the mercy of God, even we have been called and gathered into his fold as have brothers and sisters from nations around the globe. God's voice continues to echo through all the earth.

ACT

Celebrate the global nature of the Church today: Attend a service in another language. Read about what is going on in the Church in another country. Make a donation to Catholic Relief Services.

PRAY

Thank you, O God, for calling my name and welcoming me into your fold.

BEGIN

Be silent. Be still. Pray, "Come, Lord Jesus!"

PRAY

He shall defend the afflicted among the people, save
the children of the poor.

~Psalm 72:4

LISTEN

Read Matthew 1:1–17.

After the Babylonian exile, Jechoniah became the
father of Shealtiel, Shealtiel became the father of
Zerubbabel, Zerubbabel the father of Abiud. Abiud
became the father of Eliakim, Eliakim the father of
Azor, Azor the father of Zadok.

~Matthew 1:12–13

Part of a Plan Bigger Than We Know

In what remains the shortest sermon I have ever heard, I
vividly recall the parish priest of my childhood looking
up from the ambo after stumbling through the reading
of today's gospel and stating, "Children, be grateful that
your parents did not name you any of these names." He
then sat down.

Given the fear and trembling these names evoke
in pulpits near and far, it is somewhat remarkable that
the Church still insists on their being read aloud each
year. But as we enter into the octave before Christmas,
the annual proclamation of Jesus' genealogy reminds

us Jesus did not arrive on a chariot piercing the clouds but as a servant in a long lineage of servants of the Lord.

Just as the Advent season began at the "end of the story"—the kingdom of God in its fullness—the Advent season closes by going back to the beginning of the story—the kingdom of God at its start. We discover that the history of the kingdom is a history of collaboration between God and many humans who sometimes consciously yet often unwittingly lent their lives to a greater plan of which they were aware but faintly. They were royalty and simple folk, farmers and shepherds, saints and sinners. And while many longed for the kingdom, few probably had any clue as to the critical role they played in bringing it about.

Do you think it possible that God is still working this way today and using the gifts of our daily love and work in ways that we cannot imagine? On the last day, perhaps we will be as surprised as Shealtiel and Zadok to find our names read aloud by a stumbling preacher celebrating us as servants in a long line of servants of the kingdom of God.

ACT

Around the dinner table share names and stories of people in your own lives who gifted you in ways that they never knew.

PRAY

I put my life into your hands, O Lord, to use on behalf of the kingdom of God.

Sunday, December 18
Fourth Week of Advent

BEGIN

Be silent. Be still. Pray, "Come, Lord Jesus!"

PRAY

Let the Lord enter; he is king of glory

~Psalm 24:7c, 10b

LISTEN

Read Matthew 1:18–24.

This is how the birth of Jesus Christ came about.
When his mother Mary was betrothed to Joseph, but
before they lived together, she was found with child
through the Holy Spirit.

~Matthew 1:18

Compassion in the Midst of Confusion

It has long been a tradition in my family that on your
birthday those old enough to remember will tell the
story of the day you were born and the events leading
up to your birth. While the arc of the story remains the
same, details tend to vary from year to year in light of
age appropriateness and who the person is now. For no
matter how our personalities evolve, we always seem to
discover some seeds of that personality already evident
in infancy.

Each year in the days leading up to Christmas, the
Church has a similar practice of remembering Jesus'
birth story, undergirded by a similar assumption: if we
want to understand the essence of who Jesus truly is,
critical clues will already be present in the tale of his

Nativity. Only the Gospels of Luke and Matthew include such tales. In Luke's gospel, the story is told from Mary's angle on affairs. But today's gospel from Matthew preserves something of Joseph's experience. It reminds us of the complex emotions surrounding Jesus' birth, ones that will surround Jesus his whole life. Who really is this child, born to ordinary folk but conceived in mystery, swaddled in a culture trying to do what is right but breaking all the norms?

In Joseph, we meet a model of response to the confusion, doubt, and chaos that we, too, might experience when God bursts into our lives unexpectedly. When at first Joseph doesn't know what to think of Mary's pregnancy, he doesn't judge or act in anger but tries to figure out what would be the most compassionate thing to do. May the God of surprises always find in us the same impulse toward compassion.

ACT

When someone does or says something that disturbs you today, practice Joseph's nonjudgmental compassion.

PRAY

Through the intercession of St. Joseph, O Lord, teach me the art of compassion.

Monday, December 19
Fourth Week of Advent

BEGIN

Be silent. Be still. Pray, "Come, Lord Jesus!"

PRAY

Be my rock of refuge, a stronghold to give me safety.

~Psalm 41:3

LISTEN

Read Luke 1:5–25.

But the angel said to him, "Do not be afraid, Zechariah, because your prayer has been heard."

~Luke 1:13

Do Not Be Afraid

If there is any refrain that punctuates the narrative of Jesus' birth, it is this one: "Do not be afraid." Today it is spoken to Zechariah, but yesterday, Joseph heard it, as tomorrow will Mary. By the end of this week, the shepherds will hear it while watching their sheep at night. It would appear that angels of the Lord are consistently charged with speaking these words. Why? One possibility is that angels are frightening beings and whosoever encounters one is going to need to be reminded to swallow and breathe. But another possibility is that life itself can be frightening and angels tend to those moments of impenetrable depth and unfathomable height that cause us to quake: conception, birth, marriage, sickness, death. The territories into which humans nervously tread are the places where angels persistently trod. Mystery is their special domain, and to hold us upright in the face of mystery is their special mission.

Is it wrong to be afraid when life is shaped like a giant question mark? No. I imagine Jesus himself heard this refrain when the angel came to him in the garden of Gethsemane. We should hear in the angel's message less an admonition than a promise that God is with us on the edge of the unknown. That however big is the mystery in which we have found ourselves immersed, God is still bigger. Sometimes we will have experiences that take our breath away or even, as in Zechariah's case, render us speechless. But God already awaits us on the other side of confusion and awe. Just ask those who were the last in the gospels to hear the angel's refrain: the women at the tomb on Easter morn.

ACT

Talk at the dinner table with one another about what it has been like to walk through some of life's greatest mysteries in your own life journeys.

PRAY

Quell my fear before the unfathomable mysteries of life, O Lord.

Tuesday, December 20
Fourth Week of Advent

BEGIN

Be silent. Be still. Pray, "Come, Lord Jesus!"

PRAY

Who can ascend the mountain of the LORD? or who may stand in his holy place?

~Psalm 24:3

LISTEN

Read Luke 1:26–38.

And Mary said, "Behold, I am the handmaid of the Lord. May it be done to me according to your word."

~Luke 1:38

The Freedom to Say Yes

She could have said no. In God's way of doing things, there is no force, no violence, no making people do things against their will. Oh sure, there is some arm twisting: "O LORD, you have enticed me, and I was enticed," bemoans Jeremiah. But God always leaves human freedom intact. God invites us to collaborate in helping to make of this planet all that God dreams for it; God doesn't fill out our RSVP for us and put a stamp on it.

In a history in which so many humans have made such very poor choices to such devastating effect, we might wonder why God doesn't just *make* the kingdom come. Clearly God is all-powerful and can do all things. Why let the wicked, ignorant, and stubborn hold up the show? Why value human freedom so very highly?

Perhaps it is because God's very nature is love. God's very nature is friendship. And there can be no true friendship if the partners in the relationship are forced to be with one another or have an alternative motive for being together. Love isn't love unless it is freely given. God's plans for earth can't be realized unless we freely assent to them and lend our hand to them. We think that the coming of the kingdom is waiting on God to act when really God is waiting on us.

Imagine God's joy on the day of the annunciation. She could have said no, but Mary freely said yes.

ACT

> Consider: Is there something you feel God is asking your collaboration with right now? What would it take to be able to freely say yes? Talk to God about your ponderings.

PRAY

> Show me what it would mean to fully collaborate with the coming of your kingdom, O Lord.

WEDNESDAY, DECEMBER 21
FOURTH WEEK OF ADVENT

BEGIN

Be silent. Be still. Pray, "Come, Lord Jesus!"

PRAY

The LORD, your God, is in your midst, a might savior;
he will rejoice over you with gladness, and renew
you in his love.

~Zephaniah 3:17

LISTEN

Read Luke 1:39–45.

Blessed are you who believed that what was spoken
to you by the Lord would be fulfilled.

~Luke 1:45

Standing between Thomas and Mary

As the feast of Christmas rapidly approaches, we find
ourselves again sitting with a word *from* God speaking about the trustworthiness of the Word *of* God. Over
the past couple weeks, we've savored the words of the
prophets painting us a picture of the coming kingdom
of God and enjoyed words of the evangelists' testifying
to God's kingdom breaking out everywhere Jesus went.
But we live in a world that still seems far from God's
dreams being fully realized, one that sometimes makes
it hard to believe that God's Word could still have any
relevance or truth. As we mark the winter solstice—the
shortest day of the year—we may feel wrapped in darkness physically and mentally. Just where are we really
headed as a world?

For many centuries in the history of the Church, December 21 marked the Feast of St. Thomas the Apostle, a man most known for his struggle with the darkness of doubt. Although Thomas likely resents the stereotype ("Hey!" he is shouting from heaven right now, "I had *lots* of redeeming traits!"), he is forever remembered as the friend who refused to hope in the Good News of the resurrection until he saw Jesus with his own eyes. As a point of contrast, today's gospel lifts up Mary, who Elizabeth praises as one who had been able to hope in the equally improbable Good News of the incarnation even when Jesus was still only the size of a mustard seed below her heart, long before her body swelled with pregnancy.

We probably find ourselves standing somewhere in between Thomas and Mary today, and that is okay. We want to be honest about our questions, even as we are steady in our faith. Both questioning and remaining steady bear witness to a God whose Word we can count on, a God whose Word continues to shape the course of history.

ACT

Choose one kind deed you can do for another today as a way of practicing being a light in the darkness.

PRAY

Renew in me, O Lord, a deep trust in your Word.

THURSDAY, DECEMBER 22
FOURTH WEEK OF ADVENT

BEGIN

Be silent. Be still. Pray, "Come, Lord Jesus!"

PRAY

My heart exults in the LORD.

~1 Samuel 2:1

LISTEN

Read Luke 1:45–56.

He has cast down the mighty from their thrones and has lifted up the lowly. He has filled the hungry with good things, and the rich he has sent away empty.

~Luke 1:52–53

Is There a Song Growing in You?

Here is a woman who is steeped in the Word of God. We have spoken about taking time to sit with God's Word during this Advent season, allowing it to slowly work its way into our hearts. Today we glimpse the fruits of such a life in Mary. There is not one line from Mary's Magnificat that is not found earlier in scripture—in Genesis, Psalms, Job, Deuteronomy, Sirach, Micah, Samuel, Ezekiel. She has surely sat with them all, turning them over in her heart. She has traced the golden threads of God's care for the poor and hungry. She has listened to God's promises spoken over the centuries. And now, in this moment of frightful awe in the face of great mystery—a moment that could leave her speechless like Zechariah—she finds in God's Word the vocabulary she needs to express all that is going on in her own life.

Loud and clear through the hills of Judea and into the halls of history, she sings the stories and scriptures of her people in a new key.

As someone who has made a commitment to listening to and meditating on the Word of God in your own life, is there a song that has been slowly growing in you? Is there something you've discovered in your reading of scripture this Advent that helps to illumine what you are experiencing in life right now? How would you give voice to that discovery?

ACT

In a journal, write down the scripture verses that have most shaped your thinking about God's work in your own life.

PRAY

May my life be a song of praise to you, O God.

FRIDAY, DECEMBER 23
FOURTH WEEK OF ADVENT

BEGIN

Be silent. Be still. Pray, "Come, Lord Jesus!"

PRAY

Your ways, O LORD, make known to me.

~Psalm 25:4

LISTEN

Read Luke 1:57–66.

Immediately his mouth was open, his tongue freed, and he spoke blessing God. Then fear came upon all their neighbors, and all these matters were discussed throughout the hill country of Judea. All who heard these things took them to heart, saying, "What, then, will this child be?"

~Luke 1:64–66

Who Will Be the Angel?

It would be nice if an angel could show up here. The aged Elizabeth has survived childbirth. Zechariah's stunned tongue has been set free. The mysteriously-named John has arrived. And the neighbors do not know what to make of it all. Fear erupts in their hearts, perhaps a mix of curiosity and anxiety around this newborn child. Seems like a good time for a messenger of the Lord to appear and speak the angelic refrain: "Do not be afraid." But for a moment, the heavens are silent. The Lectionary opts to stop the reading without an answer to this question, perhaps to give us some time to think. What will happen if no one steps in here to quell the fear? What will become of poor John as he begins to display his unusual clothing choices and odd dietary habits? Will he be left to the gossip mill?

We live in a world filled with fear of anything or anyone unusual. Fear of immigrants. Fear of minorities. Fear of the mentally ill. Fear of people who dress and eat and think differently than us. Sometimes we perpetuate the very kind of frightful behaviors we fear by the way we treat those we do not understand. Perhaps the abrupt ending of today's gospel passage is meant to stir within us a desire to leap into the scene and make the proclamation ourselves: "Do not be afraid. God is here, too." Maybe you are the angel today's anxious world is waiting for.

ACT

Take a stand against fearmongering. Speak up when someone engages in stereotyping a group of people. Write a letter to the editor when you see an instance of fearmongering in the news. Pray for those who are a source of anxiety for you.

PRAY

O Lord, let me never be swallowed by my fears.

Saturday, December 24
Christmas Eve

BEGIN

Be silent. Be still. Pray, "Come, Lord Jesus!"

PRAY

The favors of the Lord I will sing forever.

~Psalm 89:2

LISTEN

Read Luke 1:67–79.

Zechariah his father, filled with the Holy Spirit,
prophesied, saying, "Blessed be the Lord, the God
of Israel; for he has come to his people and set them
free."

~Luke 1:67–68

The Spirit Is A-movin'

Yesterday's gospel ended with a question: "What, then,
will this child be?" Today, we hear the child's father
Zechariah—a man once mute with fear—boldly speak
his own answer to this question: This child is a prophet.
This child will preach sin and its forgiveness. Through
this child, the promises of God will be ushered in.

How does Zechariah know all this? From whence
did this newfound courage and clarity come? The first
line of today's passage names it: the Holy Spirit. The
Holy Spirit has been dancing throughout the scripture
passages we've read this week, acting as the wily collab-
orator always at work in bringing the kingdom of God
to reality through the constant giving of gifts. It is the
Spirit who overshadows Mary and brings about life. It is

the Spirit who makes Elizabeth see in Mary what no one else has yet seen. It is the Spirit who makes John leap in the womb. Always, it is the Spirit.

Sometimes we mistakenly think that the Spirit first arrived on the scene of history at Pentecost. No, the Spirit has been there all along from the dawn of creation as the wind first moved over the waters. And the Spirit flowed freely in Jesus' life from the moment of conception in the new waters of Mary's womb till the moment he exhaled one final time on the Cross. Indeed, this is the same Spirit Jesus breathed upon *us* the night of the Resurrection. And the gifts that permeated the lives of Mary and John, Zechariah and Elizabeth—the gifts of knowledge and new life, joy and understanding—are even now available to us. We need only ask.

ACT

What gifts of the Spirit—so abundantly manifest in the earliest pages of the gospels—would you want to ask for as a "Christmas gift" this year? Talk to God about the gifts you could most use in your life right now.

PRAY

Holy Spirit, come and fill me with your gifts.

Sunday, December 25

The Nativity of the Lord

BEGIN

Be silent. Be still. Pray, "Come, Lord Jesus!"

PRAY

Sing to the LORD; bless his name.

~Psalm 96:2

LISTEN

Read Luke 2:1–14.

And this will be a sign for you: you will find an infant wrapped in swaddling clothes and lying in a manger.

~Luke 2:12

Jesus, the Word of God

We've heard it so many times before that now we fail to hear anything unusual about it at all: a baby in swaddling clothes lying in a manger. For those of us who neither swaddle babies nor husband animals in our own lives, the mention of the two in the same sentence is not particularly jarring. For first-century shepherds, however, the pairing would have been thought very strange. In the time of the Roman Empire, feeding troughs were known as places where unwanted children would be abandoned. Swaddling, however, was an indicator that a child was loved and cared for. It signified a mother's presence and protection. To hear of a baby wrapped in swaddling clothes and lying in a manger would have been perplexing. Who is this child who is both loved and rejected? Who is this child whose birth is heralded by angels and yet is sleeping in a barn?

The angels say that the strangeness of the situation is a sign. It is a clue keying us in to something important about Jesus and his ministry. Throughout his whole life, he will be a contradiction: great and small, powerful and weak, loved and rejected all at the same time. Here is a man who will never be able to fit into one of our conceptual boxes. Here is one who will always surprise. Here is one who will burst our stereotypes, who will tie our imagination in knots.

Are we ready to greet a Lord like this and allow him into our lives? Has our time with the Word of God readied us to be wrapped in a mystery infinitely bigger than ourselves and find a home there? If so, Merry Christmas, and welcome to life in the kingdom of God!

ACT

Wholeheartedly welcome the Christmas feast with all of its chaos and complexities this day.

PRAY

Welcome, Lord Jesus, into my life anew.

Ann M. Garrido is associate professor of homiletics at Aquinas Institute of Theology in St. Louis, Missouri. While her first passion is teaching, for more than fifteen years she has found herself increasingly drawn to administrative roles. Garrido has served as senior editor of *Human Development Magazine* and is the author of six books, including *Redeeming Conflict* and the award-winning *Redeeming Administration*. She travels nationally and internationally doing conflict education and mediation work in both the business and church worlds. Garrido lives in Florida.